THE BEYOND WITHIN

Initiation into Mediation

by Alphonse and Rachel Goettmann

Translated by

Theodore and Rebecca Nottingham

Published by Theosis Books

www.theosisbooks.com

© 2010 by Theodore J. Nottingham

All rights reserved.

ISBN 0-9664960-9-4

Cover Art by Rebecca Nottingham

Printed in the United States of America.

TABLE OF CONTENTS

Preface

Introduction

I. WHICH PATH FOR US?

In despair on the edge of the cliff

The True Dimension of Humanity

Meditation: A Privileged Path

II. ON THE WAY TOWARD THE WAY: HOW TO MEDITATE

Sitting in meditation

The Sensation of the Divine

Meditating in the Breath of God

III. THE TRUE JOY

Asceticism: beacon on the way

If I have not love, I am nothing

You are the light of the world

Appendix I

SOME EXERCISES TO FACILITATE PROPER BREATHING

Appendix II

SUMMARY OF THE ENTRY INTO THE

FUNDAMENTAL POSTURE

PREFACE

by Theodore J. Nottingham

Out in the rolling hills of eastern France, on the edge of the German border, in a land called Alsace-Lorraine, there is a very special community known as Bethanie. It is a place of great religious activity destined to renew Christian spirituality in our day. Across Europe, seekers of the light are finding new access to the living Christ through the work of this community. Books, journals, sessions aimed at deepening our experience of the Presence of God are all part of Bethanie's mission. Hundreds have journeyed to this little out of the way place deep in the French countryside, some twenty minutes from the ancient city of Metz.

Situated on a spot of land which once housed a monastery in the seventh century, Bethanie is known as a Center of Spiritual Encounters. Its directors are Alphonse and Rachel Goettmann. He is a priest in the Orthodox Church of France, a relatively recent development in the Body of Christ which seeks to return to the earliest Traditions of the Faith. Alphonse and Rachel are themselves living examples of Bethanie's mission -- the transformation of human beings into children of God, channels of the Divine Love, new creations in Christ. Alphonse and Rachel are lovers of God, people who radiate a rare joy, humility, and unconditional affection.

They have lived a lifetime aimed at becoming receptive to the

Spirit and transparent to its expression in the world. For years they were students and close friends of Karlfried Graf Durckheim, the renowned spiritual teacher and psychotherapist who has helped untold thousands find the Christ within. (Durckheim died in December of 1988, at the age of 91, and the Goettmanns carry on his teachings while ushering them into new dimensions through their experience of the Orthodox liturgy and the wisdom of the early saints of the Church.)

Here in this quiet setting men and women learn to discover the Prayer of the Heart, that opening to the Spirit which makes possible encounters too deep for words and transforms daily life into a sacramental event. Here people become empowered to go out into the world as instruments and messengers of Unconditional Love. For the Goettmanns, it is clear that the men and women who come to drink at their wells are looking for something more than inner peace and serenity. They are looking for the Christ, the Holy One of God who has put a human face on the unknowable "I Am." There is a great hunger worldwide for spiritual awakening and Bethanie is on the cutting edge of these new horizons so vital to the future of Humanity.

To that end, the Goettmanns have published several books which are now being translated for the English-speaking world:

- *Prayer of Jesus -- Prayer of the Heart* (published by Paulist Press in the fall of 1990, then republished by Inner Life Publication in 1996, and brought out for a third edition as *The Power of the Name: The History and Practice of the Jesus Prayer* in 2009 by Orthodox Research Institute)

- *Dialogue on the Path of Initiation: An introduction to the thought of Karlfried Graf Durckheim* (republished in 2009 as *The Path of Initiation* by

Theosis Books)

- *The Spiritual Wisdom and Practices of Early Christianity* (Orthodox Research Institute (September, 2006)
- *Becoming Real: Essays on the Teachings of a Master* (Theosis Books, 2009)

The following quote from this volume offers a hint of their work and insight: "Only this complete opening to the amazing Love of God makes it possible for us to become ourselves, for we have been created to respond to this call. From it is born all fruitfulness. Transparent to God, we recognize God everywhere and in everything; we now become truly sensitive to another in his or her full reality, capable of communicating beyond impersonal appearances. Previously we could know nothing of God's purpose for t he world, but now our knowing receives its light from the Love lived in the depths of our prayer. Through our inner experience, we know that God maintains the world by the power of this Love, and wants to carry it through this Love to its fulfillment, its divinization."

During our walk around the community, Rachel rang the old church bell which echoed across the peaceful countryside. The ringing was not done to announce the top of the hour or the time of worship, but to call everyone within earshot to a remembrance of the living God. As the first colors of sunset spread across the autumn sky, we had to ready ourselves for the three hour train ride back to Paris. It was painful to leave this place whose very atmosphere seemed to sparkle with the glory of God. So much worship and so much love had transfigured a plot of land into sacred space. In that little community, made up of a few families committed to growing t gether in their common faith and sharing it with all who are on such a pilgrimage, we found a people of God bearing witness to the nearness and nurturing love of our Creator. Only that kind of daily profound transformation which makes us transparent to the Divine Love, or Being as Durckheim called it, can become a beacon for its age and all those to come.

Bethanie echoes today with the magnificent harmonies of the ancient Orthodox liturgy and the deep consciousness of lives focused on the present moment and the Presence of the Holy within in. It is a blessed place, an incubator for the regeneration of the Christian life. Its leaders are humbly living in that timeless encounter with our Creator, the experience of which is the hope of humanity.

INTRODUCTION

by Alphonse and Rachel Goettmann

This is not a book, but the utterance of a continual search verified through experience. These are the words of a life. More than thirty years ago, the decisive call came and there was no turning back: "Deep within, you are someone entirely different..." It was an explosion! But the Way still had to be found. The stages succeeded one another, but always and obstinately in the same direction: contemplative Silence. Here alone are we placed before the power of the call and the depths of its promises. We human beings are an abyss of dazzling mystery who come to self-realization only in and through contemplation, and no action can replace it.

A person's entire being and behavior depend directly and completely on this beyond within... Such a conviction came through the most personal experiences, in solitude and in the desert. It was unique. And the more it became unique, the more it opened upon the universal. Our Love, that great Silent One beyond all words of love, first showed it to us; beginning with our wedding, it has penetrated step by step toward a sharing in meditation which has never ceased. This has become our daily bread. Now we share it with hundreds of people who come from all spiritual, cultural, and geographic horizons searching for the Essential. Bethanie, Center of Spiritual Encounters located near

Metz in eastern France, is the fruit of this experience.

But if we can share today the harvest of our discoveries, it is because there was a sower: Karlfried Graf Durckheim. We have described elsewhere the adventure of our encounter with this Master and the richness of his message (*Dialogue on the Path of Initiation*). As a true Master, Graf Durckheim, far from imposing his law upon us, has opened us to our own creativity. We attempt here to enter into the understanding and experience of meditation as we practiced it with Durckheim for many years, seeking to break through the Mystery which inhabits it and calls to us as disciples of Christ. And the more we break through, the more we rejoign the living waters of Holy Scripture and the grand tradition of our Fathers!

Meditation is not only the activity of distant Asians, but the lever of all wisdom. The Orient calls the West t o this forgotten reality. Oriental wisdom can greatly enrich us in this contemplative path, on the condition that we open ourselves t o it with prudence and discernment, as did the Fathers of the Church who, in their day, knew how to make use of the best insights of Greek philosophy. They understood that all truth, wherever it appears, is a manifestation of the Word of God... This initiation into meditation is actually an initiation into humanity. It is an invitation to the Joy at the heart of a world without hope, and a call for people to rediscover their true humanity!

I

WHICH PATH FOR US?

IN DESPAIR ON THE EDGE OF THE CLIFF

Adam, where are you? On the summits of your intellect or in the depths of your being? This question is addressed to all people of all times, and to each one of us in particular.

We often look back painfully on our past or peer avidly into the future, but we always flee our today, our present moment, the only certainty of our existence. To understand what is going on, we must be aware of the fact that, from the beginning of our century, more things have happened than in the past six thousand years of written history.

We are born into a crack of time and our problems are unlike those of any previous generation. According to sociologists, there is no doubt about the absolutely exceptional phase in which humanity finds itself. Extraordinary promises stretch out before us. The scientific and technical revolution of the twentieth century could be the greatest opportunity humanity has ever had to fulfill itself. For the first time in history, we have the means of mastering our destiny. Everything points to the possibility that the stage which is to be undertaken now is as important as the first step which led humans to create tools. However, everything will depend on a radical choice. Alongside the exceptional promises are threats which are just as great . A dramatic struggle is underway between ourselves and our genius. It is up to us, with the exception of a stupid accident which is always possible, as to whether this struggle ends in the most miserable failure or opens out onto a new stage of our development. The burning question is this: will we reach a point of no return and what must we do to avoid this catastrophe?

The scientific revolution, which has become a technical one, is out of control. First oriented toward the natural world, it now surrounds us, envelops us, and has suddenly penetrated into the depths of our hearts through the flood of mass media, finally reaching into our very genes with the power to transform us biologically. For the first time, we are in a phase of history where our progress threatens our existence. What now? Disintegration? New beginning? Metamorphosis? Adam, where are you?...In despair! We are cut off from our secret intimacy with the cosmos. Little by little, we have transformed our planet into an immense factory which exploits matter and energy. Pushed on by a blind and disordered instinct, we condemn it to pillage, poisoning, and ruin. Never before have we so assaulted our environment. Nature is dying, boxed into national parks where our descendants will come and see what forests once looked like. Thousands of species have already disappeared. The reality which was the condition of humanity for centuries is now collapsing. Will we be able to survive all alone?

Cut off from the cosmos, we now evolve in an apocalyptic universe: how many have already fallen beneath the mushroom cloud and how many more fall at this very moment beneath the concentrations of radioactive dust creating all sorts of infirmities and cancers? The food chain is polluted, mutations in germinal cells are probable. Having become a stumbling robot, we are going insane and, to protect ourselves, we are arming ourselves in a demented way. This is plunging us into the cruelty of wars, a universe of genocide and aggression where, as Helder Camara says, is dropped the most catastrophic of all bombs: the M bomb, the explosion of misery! Technical civilization exerts on us many pressures from earliest childhood and, in the weakest among us, creates psychopaths, drug addicts, and even criminals. Humanity is crushed by the products it has fabricated.

Machines are part of our biological life like the shell of a snail, but we are snails who are being crushed by our shells while still creating them. The condition of our existence then becomes pathological. Exposed, uprooted, and without refuge, we fall into a chaotic multiplication of needs, a neurosis for material comfort and an impossibility of living without mass communication, especially television. This is an imbalance of Nature, and for some, an irreversible current. Beneath the overdevelopment of human power with its increase of abundance and leisure lies an incredible emotional, psychological and moral underdevelopment . The effort toward a scientific society has no t worked. We are giving up on the illusion that science holds the key to all our problems. Not only do we no longer dominate our environment, but we have lost the lever of our inner universe.

The mechanical organization of existence has reduced everything to servitude and destroyed t hat which cannot fit into its structures. It begets a common sinking into the superficial and the indifferent. And we are now becoming aware of the irreparable loss of substance which has taken place. The issue is not the condemnation of technology or science, but to point out that, without consciousness, they are blind and drunken and destroy humanity. We are losing ourselves in what should be a means rather than an end. The era of the computer can only lead to a new age of civilization if we rediscover and hold tightly to our true aims. Technical advance yes, but by whom and for what? It is our identity which is the issue, the interpretation of a certain image we have of ourselves which is the source of all our ills. The best observers seem to agree today on this point: the underdevelopment of humanity, the deficiency of our being, and our inner misery are the common denominator of all our various underdevelopments: psychological, physiological and material. It is in our very being that we are sick!

Let us not fall once more into new hypotheses which might make us feel better. Humanity is amputated from its essential interiority, its deep roots, and the mystery of its vital center. For those who know how to see, there is visible, beneath our masks and appearances, the diseases of the soul and the spirit. What must we do? From everywhere, we are projected to the surface, pulverized and reduced to mechanics. The snail is crushed by its shell, yet continues to create it... From the moment we value human beings by their capacity to produce, the individual loses his or her uniqueness. We then cease to be ourselves and fall into the functional. Here we are objectified, torn from the depths which make us truly human, transparent to our being and opened to the inner source from which we can continually receive ourselves. For the world, to be is to be adapted to objectivity, accepting to reduce our mysterious and immense consciousness, and to function only in the collective and the general.

We have abandoned our heart to be dominated by our mind. Reason without the heart is unreasonable! Can we have a tree without its roots? The House of humanity is divided, and we live only in the attic. The vast resources of being remain unused and are drying up in a spiritual void. The rationalization of daily life on all levels continually bludgeons Life in its very essence, and we exist in the restricted spaces of abstraction and superficial conduct. What is the point of furnishing my attic if the roof keeps me from standing up? We have identified ourselves with our rational self and let the most important part of ourselves fall into the night of the subconscious. Each one of us can notice that, as we age, we leave behind that original wholeness which radiates from the little child and we become increasingly strangers to ourselves. Except for certain privileged hours of our life, it is very rare that we correspond with who we are in our depths, present to ourselves and our surrounding, that we reach our true capacities, t hat we become authentic. We always remain outside of our own reality.

Most of the time, the experience we have of ourselves does not include who we really are. In the same way, there is an abyss between the experience we have of our environment and what that environment actually is. The thing itself, as Kant said, remains a stranger to us, closed in on itself; we only see appearances. This is where many of our conflicts and confusions come from. Little by little we are led to decomposition, dragging with us the rotting of an entire civilization and the crumbling of religion. The reduction of humanity to its rational and objectifying "self," exclusively functional and utilitarian, has introduced a great schism within us. The unity of being is broken and the consciousness of belonging to an undivided All, the openness toward t he beyond within us, where we are originated and receive ourselves, is lost. Our anchoring is no longer in the Absolute.

Divided within and consequently separated from the rest of the universe of which we were in a way the summary, cut off from the Source of life, we have turned toward our "little self" living on the surface of things. And the unlimited field of our mystery becomes a tiny prison in which, alone, we end up adoring ourselves! Uncentered from God, concentrated on ourselves, we make ourselves the ultimate purpose of life. The spirit cut off from God and no longer nourished by Him, feeds on the soul. But finding only emptiness there where God communicated the fullness of life, the soul in turn cannibalizes the body and seeks the pleasures of the flesh. The body itself, now a desecrated Temple and no longer dwelling in the Holy of Holies, is literally thrown out, extraverted through its pores and its five senses, and delivered to avarice and possessiveness.

Everything is done through the deformed and deforming prism of this disintegrated autonomy, the objectifying and rational consciousness. It only sees by ascertaining, that is, by fixing in a static state all living reality, projecting it out of its mystery toward the dead abstraction of concept, reducing it to a useful object. The reaction is always immediate: as soon as our senses come in contact with something, they classify it, define it, tag it: "doctor"... "laborer"..."peasant"..."flower"..."plane"... good"..."bad"..."cold"... "hot"... We see only the superficial. It is a horizontal view in which everything is separated, opposed, broken. The inner sight, rooted in the luminous depths of Being, uncovers not o nly the appearances, the visible form, but "that which informs the form," and reveals how "all is in each thing and each thing is in all," as a wave is the concentration of the entire ocean. This is true seeing. Our ordinary consciousness is isolated, windowless, veils everything through the mental screen, knows only itself and filters all reality, which is so stupendous in its invisible dimension.

From the days of the prophets, such persons have been recognized for their "lack of depth" and their "lack of roots" to the extent that they "see without seeing, hear without hearing, for their heart (their inner center) is hardened" (Mtt 13). In other words, all relationships are falsified: with oneself, with others, with the world, with God. This is perversion in the truest sense: "spirit -soul-body" becomes "body-soul-spirit"...Not only is their direction inversed, but their unity is lost. This is the disposition which treats t he self as absolute, as an end in itself, and therefore uses everything to satisfy it and augment its power. This is not simply a bad temperament, but the fundamental inauthenticity of a divided consciousness with no direction in the midst of arbitrary impulses, given over to brokenness and error, a self capable of inventing the hydrogen bomb and concentration camps for whoever does not kneel before it...

The more this affirmation of the self increases in power, and that is its tendency in each moment, the more it falls into division, dualism, rupture: I separate myself from others. But this inflation of self depends on others, on their manipulation. This is a complete change of perspective, an inner alienation which is called original sin, not only because it

was committed at the dawn of some distant past, but because I commit it every day and it cuts me off from my deeper identity, there where I originate, and because of this, all my efforts, even the most insignificant, are aborted from the place of their birth. The person who has lost his or her identity is like the stream that has lost its source: the stream becomes a pond for ducks, muddy and stagnating.

It has ceased to be a stream and lost its joy whose nature is to receive the surging life of the source. It is still water, but for how long? Amputation...Exile...Wandering far from our vitalizing Source...The mundane self never ceases to be seduced by the fruits of the Tree of Knowledge, that is, by self-idolatry. We want to become gods through our own efforts and not through the Tree of Life which is God. It is the story of the stream and its source, humanity's supreme attempt against all Covenant with anything other than itself. This has nothing to do with the legends of certain catechisms or the moral of bad sermons. "To sin," in one of its etymological meanings, means to miss the mark, to have the wrong aim, and therefore to miss the goal.

Persons who are cut off from their roots in the divine, from the beyond within, live only in the reduced dimensions of time and space (the horizontal dimension) with the reduced consciousness of the "little self." They have ceased to be persons and are now merely individuals. They have lost their essential dimension, beyond time and space, the one which constitutes them as persons. Can such people ever find happiness?

Meister Eckhart has left us a picture, which defies all logic, of the inexpressible happiness which rises in persons who recover their true identity: "*God takes such pleasure in this similitude or identity, that he pours out his nature and his whole being. His pleasure is as great as a horse let loose in a flat plain that gallops as fast as he can because that is his nature and pleasure. So it is with God. It is his pleasure and rapture to discover someone's true identity because he can place his whole nature in it, being himself this identity.*"

We have said that humanity is sick in its very being. This despair is collective only because it is within each one of us.

At the same time, we continue to seek to remedy our distress on t he external level. Cut o ff from our source, we find ourselves before a void from which rise three great sufferings, the three fundamental distresses of human beings, the immediate consequences of our inner rupture, and the common denominator of all our ills:

- the fear of death,

- the meaninglessness of life,

- solitude.

First of all, this enormous security in which we envelop ourselves, from the house with its many gadgets to the most sophisticated weapons to defend our borders, reveals the fundamental anguish of humanity seeking to stand on its own strength and to overcome its fear of annihilation. Pulled back into the domain of our egotistical little self, having burned

the bridges with the rest of creation and with our Creator, we feel ourselves always threatened in our acquired positions. Fragile and ephemeral, they must be defended against all adversity in the midst of a hostile world. Then a terrible anguish of not being able to live settles into the soul like a corrosive substance. Death is at the end of the journey but can already be seen on the street corner.

Like the pond which is no longer connected to its source and therefore goes nowhere, humanity cut off from its Creator, while aspiring toward him with its whole being, sees this aspiration crumble in disgust: our life makes no sense, everything is meaningless.

More fearsome than total destruction, whether atomic or biological, is the total absence of meaning. Money, power, prestige, all the ridiculous worldliness of a self ever more greedy in its never satisfied aspiration toward something undefined leads only to the psychiatrist, suicide, drugs, boredom, and indifference.

The moment I identify with my little self, I enter into a world of division. I am fixed and limited; my self has precise boundaries which can only lead to grim solitude. All modem art, literature, and cinema are filled with this reality. The more we slip into the pride of rationality, the more we find ourselves alone and thrown into the inability to communicate.

The anguish before death, the absurdity of life, and solitude are the three aspects of the metaphysical distress of humanity. There is no worry, no problem or suffering which does not originate there. And, in the end, the only question we carry within, however unconscious and repressed it may be, is: "How can I be freed from this despair?" This question underlies all that we do, from the least to the greatest act; it is the secret engine of all our initiatives and plunges us into a sort of mysterious expectation for something else which should be coming-and yet never shows up! If a liberation exists, it can manifest itself only at the heart of our triple suffering:

•• power in anguish,

•• light in meaninglessness,

•• love in solitude.

In the end, original sin is also our original opportunity, allowing us to rediscover the paradise lost of our depths, our Promised Land within, if only we will consent to leave our self-imposed exile and undertake the long journey through t he desert of our alienation. We are at the turning point of history. As in the Middle Ages, we must once again break through the fog of our downfall and of our travesty. There will be a new beginning only through the return to our essence, there where our genesis takes place and where we can rediscover our true birth.

THE TRUE DIMENSION OF HUMANITY

Prisoners of our distress and anguish, we forever repress our deeper being. From this searing suffering, though it remains inexplicable to ordinary consciousness, can be born an immense yearning for something we do not know and yet which lives within us.

A certain agitation, feelings of fear, guilt, and inner emptiness become our habitual companions. They are there without apparent motive, and nothing in the world can remedy them: all our security measures leave that fear untouched; not one of our accumulated riches can fill the emptiness always widening within; and the honest person who leads a life without reproach continues to feel a strange guilt.

Through this yearning, we secretly feel a liberating plenitude beyond all possession, all power, all knowing that reduce our self to mundane futilities. We sense the possibility of becoming someone utterly different through a never ending transformation and through the existence of meaning beyond all meaning and meaninglessness, beyond all justices and injustices as understood by our reason. We sense the existence of a love beyond all particular love, independent and capable of begetting true independence.

This yearning for the Infinite which nothing can satisfy is the sign of Something Else. But this beyond is never a someplace else: it is in our depths. Yet these depths cannot be reached by our rational consciousness which measures and defines. We simply feel it, sense it. It is an intuition of Being which has nothing in common with the logic of the objectifying self and all that it grips onto. This intuition becomes stronger and more demanding as it generates a new consciousness, not in our reason but in our hearts.

We then begin to take seriously those short, privileged moments of life which leave us with an unforgettable memory: the day, the hour, the place where the presence of Being has come through like lightning and forever marked our memories. Each one of us remembers these luminous points which are strewn across our existence. Suddenly and unexpectedly, unrelated to anything, we are transplanted into a dazzling reality which is absolutely other. This may last only seconds, yet we know that a dimension which has nothing to do with space and time has just touched us.

The occasion is sometimes insignificant, and such an experience often comes to us when we reach the extreme limit of our reason and face the walls of our little self. We are drowned in the night of despair. At that moment, we can be literally seized by the light and find ourselves projected beyond all anguish, meaninglessness, or solitude!

The danger is to stop at this experience and say "it was beautiful!" without having become conscious of what it was all about. Only a memory will remain-when it actually was a call toward another shore: for an instant we have been revealed as completely other, who we truly are, and who we are called to become.

All our happiness depends on our response to this call. This is the great difference between the tendency of the East and that of the West: in the West, we seek to master the external conditions of life; in the East, we search for the path leading toward inner maturity. Western culture rests in part on rational knowledge and on a supernatural revelation which is often only intellectually adhered to . The East, not knowing such a revelation and having never considered reason as the valid means of investigating reality and meaning, turned toward inner experience. Taken seriously, inner experience became a source of life and a path to wisdom. For the West, far removed from its source, the East can be the star which will someday awaken it from its lethargy. For Christians who do not know the essentials of their faith, the East can be a call to the best of their own Tradition: a permanent invitation to truths which they have too often accepted only intellectually or have rejected for the same reasons.

The younger generations are aware of all this. It is as though what was once the privilege of a few is taking hold of great numbers now. There is talk of a chaotic "rush toward t he soul." The foundations of the God of Reason have cracked: the rise of sects, the great movement for the development of human potential, and the schools for the expansion of consciousness, along with groups dealing with transcendental initiation, the devotees of Krishna, Moon, and many others. It's enough to take your breath away! Then there is also Yoga and Zen, and the charismatic renewal. But even if they all seek something similar, they are far removed from what we are sharing here.

We ought not be too optimistic about this phenomenon. The risk is enormous: putting new wine into old wine sacks! This condemns the wine to turn bad. Often, the proposed experience actually veils the reality which the candidate aspires toward with his or her whole being! And since it is known only as an aspiration, as an inexpressible yearning, the seeker is not a good judge in the matter. The path may be doomed to sink into exercises of liberation of self through the self in a worship of inner dissolution, the seeming benefits of the relaxation of the tensions of the little self, but ending only in the no man's land of a superficial self without boundaries. Or seekers discover in the powers of being a good opportunity for self-importance. They attribute to themselves powers which come from a place they know nothing about, and t hey fall into pride: they are now at the other extreme of a spiritual experience which reveals us to ourselves and shows us our relationship to our Creator. This is enough to keep anyone from being born to a new consciousness and doom us to wander about indefinitely in the deceit of poor imitations!

There is, however, something promising occurring in the West, there where we begin to perceive and to verify an entirely different vision of humanity. It is not only in the proliferation of mystical groups that this is manifested, but also in a certain philosophy of life and the great current of new psychotherapies which are beginning to seriously rock the foundations of Freudian assumptions. On his deathbed, C.G. Jung was enthused by his reading of Eastern mystics and had the feeling that he could have said the same thing they were saying!

But the great pioneer and master of this therapy which makes it a wisdom is Karlfried Graf Durckheim. After more than half a century of research and experience, of profound assimilation of oriental and western culture, of long practice with thousands of disciples from around the world, and of confrontation with his scientific discipline, he summarized his position at the end of his life in this way:

If you asked me today to express in one sentence the core of my teaching, I would answer: taking seriously the double origin of man, celestial and earthly. The West has forgotten it. In believing that the celestial was the exclusive realm of faith, and that only

the earthly could be the object of practice and experience, the West has frustrated man in his spiritual development. Yet, the celestial origin of man is part of his essential being. Man participates in the depths of his being with the divine Being and can become conscious of it in particular experiences. It is the experience of an unconditioned reality as opposed to the conditioned reality of the existential self and its world. Man is a citizen of two worlds: the one of existential reality, limited by time and space, accessible to reason and to his powers, and the one of essential reality which is beyond time and space, accessible only to our inner consciousness and inaccessible to our powers. The destiny of man is to become the one who can witness to transcendental Reality at the very heart of existence. To achieve this, we must first learn to take seriously the great experiences through which, in privileged moments, Being touches us and calls to us. Ibis is the fundamental meaning of all spiritual experience as I understand it: to open ourselves to being seized by our essential being through experiences which manifest it, and to increasingly develop a way of life which allows us to witness to Being in every moment.

The double origin of man is thus opened to experience. It represents the source, the promise, and the fundamental work of man, whose basis is awakening to the experience of Being. It seems to me that the hour has come when the West awakens to an experience of Being and to a practice of the Way which is not a privilege of the East alone but can become, on the contrary, the opportunity and the condition for a truly human religion. (Cited in La Vie Spirituelle, number 592, p. 724).

e find in these few lines a clear grasp of that which is best in the ancient Christian Tradition. But it has taken the struggle of a lifetime to rediscover it under the ruins of the enormous distraction which has overwhelmed us since the Renaissance! And the battle is far from being won: will the representatives of most churches accept a foundation other than their dogmatic systems of thought? Spiritual experience finds its place there with great difficulty. And for good reason! The knowledge which it brings and the action to which it leads are of a radically different nature than objective knowledge and doctrinal elaborations. It is not that these turn away from the inner life; on the contrary, they even make it their object of study. But in doing so they inhibit its advent. In other words: reason does not have access to things which it debates. To think about interiority is to move in the realm of opposites and dualism which the inner experience invites us to leave in order for it to take place. That is its condition: a reversal of attitudes.

Master D.T. Suzuki said one day to Durckheim: "Western knowledge looks toward the outside, Eastern wisdom looks toward the inside. But if we look within in the way that we look without, we make of the inside an outside." We objectify, we fix things in a static state, and that which is alive goes away. This is the tragedy not only of a certain theology or ecclesiastical practice, but of the whole of classical psychology and of the structures of education which are founded upon it.

Durckheim extended Suzuki's insights and added that it is absolutely vital to know how to look out side the way we should look inside, making of the outside an inside!

This would profoundly change our relation to the world, to things and to ourselves. Our references would then be based on the most direct experience. Obviously, we cannot avoid receiving such an experience through images and formulating it in words, objectifying it in some way. This is vital if we hope to communicate the experience. That is not the problem! All religions have sought to formulate in a coherent way their first experience. What is often forgotten afterward is that this formulation does not deliver its contents through a simple lecture or through rational comprehension, but only to the one who in turn makes it his or her experience. Otherwise, we are reduced to external approaches, to instruments of analysis or interpretation; and that which was, at its origin, an invitation to live something extraordinary, to follow a path of discovery, becomes a quarrel of schools, a paper chase for diplomas, theoretical arguments, or a pretext to swell up our "little self." This is hardly a caricature of what has happened to Christianity!

Without being reborn on another level of consciousness beyond the rational self, we do not enter into living contact with this reality whose quality and significance are radically new, that is to say, of which we can have no idea based on our own ideas (Ephesians 3:20). That is why conversion, the great turning around leading to the death of the ego, is the key to every biblical message as well as to all other religions. We are each invited into an amazing experience: "Come and see" (John 1:39). It is the turning point of life which finally gives us "ears to hear, eyes to see, and a heart to understand" (Matthew 13: 13-15).

Concretely speaking, what is this experience which reveals our true dimension? First of all, it is an experience of the being which we are in our depths, beyond all image and concept. And, because it is inseparably linked to it, this is also an experience of absolute Being. But often Being is neutral to begin with, impersonal, unnamable transcendence, a burning bush escaping all the usual categories of ordinary consciousness and invariably answering its first solicitations with: "I Am Who I Am" (Exodus 3:14). In any case, the inner explosion is overwhelming and the fire all consuming.

In his Metaphysical Journal, Gabriel Marcel relates the following: *"I no longer doubt. Miraculous joy this morning. I have for the first time clearly experienced grace. These words are frightening, but that is what it is -- and I am submerged. Blessed submersion. But I don't want to write more. And yet, I feel the need to. This is truly a birth. Everything is different."* Examples like this are many and varied, but it is always the same event: the abrupt breakthrough of Being in our ordinary existence. The phenomenon can be more or less profound, an ephemeral touch, or an enormous shaking. Accordingly, Durckheim speaks of a sensation of Being or an experience of Being. We have said that each of us has some memory of this kind of sensation, even if it is not spectacular and we have not attributed much importance to it . Durckheim wrote in his The Way of Transformation:

We suddenly feel ourselves in a strange ambiance. We are entirely present, completely there, and yet not focused on anything in particular. We feel ourselves in a very peculiar way, without harshness, harmonious within ourselves, and very open. Because of this openness, a profound fullness emerges. We are both absent and present, overflowing with life. We rest within ourselves and we discover an inner affinity with everything that surrounds us. We are united to everything, yet detached from everything. We feel

ourselves incredibly guided and yet free from all obligation; poor in this world but covered with riches and inner power.

This is a participation in Being. The certainty that I am fully myself and that "I Am the One Who Is" arises from the same creative act in this point where the two join together .But this sensation of Being is often only a preparation, the messenger of the experience of Being which is overwhelming and liberating in another way. When our human distress reaches an impossible paradox, and our way of living becomes an attitude of surrender, we then open ourselves to an invasion from beyond.

This has often been seen in the depths of despair, in the terrifying anguish of death or annihilation. There again the experiences are many: situations where death is close, bombings or wars, serious illness, accidents. Fear is at its height, death is inevitable, the last defenses of the little self are about to crumble. If at t hat precise moment, we consent to lose our acquired positions and accept the unacceptable, we are suddenly invaded by a prodigious peace, freed from all fear and absolutely unassailable by death, however near it may be. For this living "thing" has taken hold of us, an indescribable Power and Fullness which have nothing to do with death; we find ourselves in an entirely different dimension. We are another person.

The same experience is even better known among those who find themselves at the extreme limits of an absurd situation, plunged into the meaninglessness of life, when no remedy is possible. Situations of terrible injustices, inhuman treatment, senseless conditions of life-times when resignation and rebellion would be dead ends. Being able to accept the unacceptable, that is to say, consenting to leave behind ordinary consciousness, is to be suddenly transfigured by a Light which transcends absurdity or meaninglessness. It is a deeper meaning, beyond all meaning and meaninglessness, an in conceivable inner order.

Other distresses which can provoke this experience of Being occur when we are thrown into complete solitude: the loss of someone very close to us, being excluded from a community, or total isolation. Let this reality penetrate you and say "yes" to the impossible pain, if only for a few seconds. This can introduce you to a Love beyond all limits of time and place. We then feel ourselves vitalized from within, surrounded at the heart of solitude, deeply connected to others, closer to them than ever before.

Every time this dimension seizes us, it reveals its Trinitarian character. Everyone knows that the richest man in the world is also the saddest! This comes from having lost his roots. The person who recognizes the essence of this agony discovers the ultimate secret of all his desires: to live fully, realizing his personhood and rediscovering unity. This is why we long for Being when we are cut off from it. Whether we are conscious of this or not, always and everywhere we discover ourselves and t he world under this triple aspect. All reality, all that lives, is animated, penetrated, centered in the Trinity of Being, and nothing either in humanity or in the universe is outside of this key to everything:

- The Source which gives Life: that which lives does not live through itself, but receives Power and Fullness from Being which wants to give itself and manifest itself in existence.

Closed off from this creative source, we necessarily fall into agony and insecurity, the fear of death.

- The Word which gives Form: that which lives realizes itself in its particular form and becomes itself. It is the meaning of life, the

Light of Being which seeks to manifest itself in a different image through every creature. The refusal to do so leads to the fall into meaninglessness.

- The Breath which gives Harmony and Movement: it leads all that lives beyond and through all differentiation toward the Totality and Unity of Being in which all participate. This energy re-creates unity within us and within all that surrounds us, taking us out of solitude and division. We are then transfigured.

This experience of the Trinity of Being is a "leap into a new kind of consciousness, a rebirth in the roots of man," according to Durckheim. The old self dies; a new being which has discovered its true center appears. Opposites are abolished, dualism is overcome, subject-object converge. This is the epiphany of Life so hoped for and awaited in the concrete existence of each one of us, as Christ revealed and promised it: creative Force of the Father, Light of the Son, vivifying Energy of the Spirit. In coming to heal the wounds of humanity, God reveals a triple face. Desperate humanity longs for the Divine Trinity -- to such an extent that if one o f the three Presences were to vanish, life would no longer be possible.

Since these statements completely escape the control of reason, we can question the credibility of such experiences. Are they not illusions or projections of a completely subjective sentimentalism? What are the criteria which allow us to recognize that this is truly an experience of another dimension, an experience of Being? The old spiritual traditions have discerned many, the most important being the birth of a certain taste, the radiance of persons who come out of an experience of Being, especially their transformation, not forgetting the intervention at t hat very moment of the Demon, the Adversary of life and of all spiritual progress.

We first experience a particular taste which occurs when we come in contact with people and things, a kind of intuition of the numinous diffused everywhere. The numinous is a superior quality which indicates to us the presence of another reality, completely different from the one that falls immediately under our senses, a quality which we can perceive in all that surrounds us, especially in moments when the phrase "it's beautiful!" no longer suffices to express what we feel. It is not simply a qualitative or superlative word. Teilhard de Chardin has written wonderful pages on this diaphany of Being in the world:

I had truly acquired a new sense, the sense of a new quality or dimension. Deeper still: a transformation had occurred within me in the very perception of being. Being had now become in some way tangible, tasty. Coming through all the forms which he puts on, being itself began to attract and intoxicate me. A Universal Smile coming from the heart of things ... the first shiver perceived from the world animated by the Incarnation ..incandescent inward layers within each life. (The Divine Milieu)

At such times, we always experience fullness and unity to the extent that our deeper consciousness is awakened. These are powerful experiences, sometimes causing overwhelming fascination, sometimes simple sparks of wonder. Those who live with the Psalms are filled with this mysterious Presence everywhere perceptible and make of it their nourishment. For them, the whole of creation becomes a place of communion with God, for there is nothing which is not the expression of God's glory and the receptacle of God's Breath (Psalm 104).

The second criterion, that of exceptional radiance of the one who is opened to Being, is just as astonishing. It has nothing in common with the natural light which emanates from our ordinary moods and our mundane joys. Nor is it the false radiance which comes from a strong personality where the self leaves no room for Being. But rather it is a profound transparence which lets appear a Force of another order and gives rise to an atmosphere of a particular character, indefinable, manifesting the presence of Life in all its freshness and purity. Since this is not a matter of a localized optical phenomenon, the objectifying consciousness cannot grasp it. Only the one who is himself transparent to Being can be touched by it. "He who participates with the divine energy," says Gregory Palamas, "becomes himself, in some way, the Light; he is united to the light and with the Light." This is infinitely more than a simple criterion of verification. The reality of the Light, known to all religions, is so inherent in all Orthodox theology and liturgy that they are impossible without it.

This leads us to the third criterion, which is transformation: the Light is nothing else than the visible character of God who communicates himself to us in order to lead us to our own deification. "You will be as gods," say the Holy Scriptures. Transformation is the best argument in witnessing to the truth of the experience of this other dimension o f humanity. We cannot accuse someone of sentimental subjectivism or of illusion when he or she has been completely changed through the experience of Being and now lives a radically new life, profoundly liberated from obsession with death, the meaninglessness of life, and solitude.

But this transcendent reality is not just a liberation from our despair. It is also a permanent questioning of all our acquired positions and of all our fixations, a complete reversal of our values, an abolition of all false securities, and a reconsideration of our way of life. A new dimension must appear which nothing can wall up and which has nothing to do with ordinary consciousness. It is not even the summit of this consciousness, but rather another consciousness altogether: a consciousness-vision which does not divide or oppose, but which ties everything together in a single bundle.

This unity of vision is the unity of Being, and through that the conquest of time and space. The infinite is then seen in the finite of things and all eternity in the passing second. Each instant is an absolute, a complete whole, a beatitude. The opposite is the constant projection into the future or pull toward the past of a mind which is never present, tossed about by hopes and regrets. It is the same for space: everything is a totality for this new consciousness; engendered by the Absolute, it discovers the Absolute everywhere and is in turn recognized by this inexpressible Reality. This is wonder. At the center of the least object, infinite immensity which contains everything is unveiled.

MEDITATION: A PRIVILEGED PATH

It is in this context of life and death that we must trace a path. We are at the crossroads. And the decision for the journey can come only from persons or communities who have become aware of the depths of their being and are present to t he adventure of the twentieth century. Both must be held together, for this is not the time to run away in search of mystical comforts. The inner life is not a decadent complacency of the self or "bourgeois" luxury. We must look directly in the face of the realities of our time!

But how is this possible? Many believe that it is already too late to humanize the inhuman forces at work among us. In the light of historical facts as well as of our widespread neurosis, there is indeed no convincing reason to believe in the advent of a sudden mental mutation which would allow us to bring about an entirely different future. There are some who hope that biological progress will soon synthesize a hormone or an enzyme which will be able to heal our paranoid dispositions.

Will the salvation of humanity come out of laboratories? Will it appear on the shelves of pharmacies and be picked out by consumers? The day may not be far off when we will add the elixir of a mental stabilizer to drinking water so as to lower criminal behavior, to enhance the coordination of neurological circuits, to lessen conflict, and to normalize things.

But this would be criminal in itself, transmuting humans into passive robots. It would be naive to hope that drugs could regenerate the spirit, introducing something that was not already there. A revolution of an entirely different order is needed because humanity is of a different order, and if we now face our greatest threat, we will be able to conquer it only by acts which are equally without precedence. Before such an extraordinarily new danger we need to find the source of the original and true creative power.

Today, we must rediscover ourselves in all our dimensions. Humanity's most heroic adventure is not the exploration of our external universe, however infinite it may be, but the journey toward our true nature. Infinity is found within us. Only from there will the world be re-created, for that is its origin: the inner force of humanity!

To survive, humanity needs a spiritual revolution. All the greats of our century converge around this point, believers and unbelievers alike. Nietzsche's Zarathustra was not the product. of a degenerate imagination but the first to observe that humanity must rise above itself. Einstein insisted on the transformation of human life in its totality, the necessity for conversion. Jaspers, another agnostic, went even further and did not hesitate to state that everything comes from the individual and depends on him. We have no other power than to draw from the liberty which rests in our depths. To dare to be an individual is to become transfigured in our relationship with our inner freedom, or, for believers, in our relationship with God. The emphasis here is not on the isolation of the self but on the intensity, the passionate interest of the self's relationship with God (or its being, its freedom), and through God, with others and the world.

This requires a permanent watchfulness. The place of this accomplishment is meditation, the kind which we will be describing here, exposing us to both the incessant movement of transformation within and genuine encounter with the outer world. This dialectic must be held together, otherwise we fall into a kind of suffocation of the self by the self or into a destructive rationalism. We might call it "active wisdom," liberating the extraordinary potential of our spiritual forces and finally letting surface all the happiness which inhabits us already.

This is what meditation aims at: creating a living person who sees God. The human being's masterwork is himself or herself. The word *meditation* does not mean here a reflection on a theme or on some rational thought process. Meditation is understood here as a *path of transformation*. It is a maturation of the entire person: in our relationship to ourselves; in our relationship to others and to the world; in our relationship to God; in the transfiguration within us of Absolute Being.

We therefore take the word meditation in its literal sense, *meditari (itari in medio)*, which means being led toward the center. The center is not something toward which we concentrate, but something which concentrates us, uniting us from within, toward t he interior. This center is essential Being, our transcendent kernel which is felt as a state in which the opposition of subject-object is dissolved. Such a state of relaxation is followed by the sensation of the birth of a new form. This is how essential Being itself makes its entry into our consciousness and is felt there as the vital center of a new awareness of the world. We feel as though we are newly born. Karlfried Durckheim. tells us that "this contact with Being begins with an almost unconscious yearning of the heart and must be followed ceaselessly, until we reach the fundamental experience of the explosion of self and the realization of Being, which transforms everything."

II

ON THE WAY TOWARD THE WAY:

HOW TO MEDITATE

SITTING IN MEDITATION

Since the secret of Self and God is "absolutely unlike any idea we may have created" (Berdiaev), all platonic meditation is doomed to failure. Many have "meditated" their entire lives, as much as an hour a day, and yet they find themselves in their old age full of bitterness. "They are spiritually sick. Far from being empty themselves, they are full; they become angry as soon as their self-centered interests are touched or threatened. They seek vengeance for the wrong that has been done to them because they are burdened with an I which can be injured" (Merton). That kind of meditation or prayer is a narcissism which does not know itself, a perversion of the spirit, or simple cerebral sensuality comforting the old man in his unconscious refusal of the Gospel. This is not the Path of transformation.

Meditation can only be an exercise of the whole person, in which nothing escapes the call to conversion, not even the least cell of the body. Everything must work toward t he transparence to Being and prepare itself to die so that it may be transfigured by It. Here, extremes touch and interpenetrate each other--the person is one. To join with our extreme interiority, at the very edge of the mysterious source of life in order to receive it, is not an abandonment of the exterior world but its integration. It is here that everything begins, through the body that I am. The body is not an object, but our way of being present: in this sense, I am my body because it is my expression in the world, my capacity to achieve the original unity in which opposites are melted down so that we may reach beyond all soul-body duality in order to live in a new dimension. Therefore, everything in our life takes root in our corporal experience. All that expresses balance, movement and creativity, especially when it is a matter of the advent of Life itself, all things which are the condition of being human respect the laws written in the flesh.

In this sense, it is striking that the Bible does not even have a word to describe the body as separated from the rest! Unity is such that there is no modification of the body without a modification o f the spirit and vice versa as saint Basil said so strongly in the fourth century. The three essential functions which allow the body the realization of unity are: right attitude, appropriate tension, and breathing. It is through these that we enter into meditation. This is when there exists the possibility of transparence. At the dawn of human wisdom, we find Patanjali and the Buddha sitting in lotus position. It has been said that this way of sitting is humanity's most inspired discovery. It allows people of all times and of all traditions to realize that for which they were born.

Despite appearances, there is nothing oriental about it. It is so appropriate to universal humanity that as soon as the little rational self is no longer at the center, people will want to sit t his way. This explains why the mentally retarded, for instance, spontaneously take this position and that western mystics appropriate it without having learned it. On the other hand, to t he intellectual person, it always offers the opportunity for an absolutely privileged path. This way of sitting allows a total immobility for a length of time, an utter letting go, and the experience of a rebirth from within the vital center. However, the exterior form of the lotus position is only an indication. Right sitting, or the fundamental posture, is not at all linked to the rigor of that position!

The most important factor is that the backbone be straight, and the knees lower than the pelvic region. With that in mind, one can sit in many different ways which are as traditional as the lotus position. "Each will choose that which will be most appropriate for him," said Theophan the Recluse. He added that "the attention of the soul depends also on a suitable position of the body."

THE LOTUS:

Sit on a cushion or a folded blanket, legs stretched out before you. Take t he right foot and place it, with the soul of the foot facing upward, on the left thigh, then do the same with t he left foot. Both knees should touch the floor.

THE HALF-LOTUS:

As with the lotus, except that only one of the feet is placed on the opposite thigh while the other rests on the floor in front of it.

THE CUP:

Here the legs are not crossed but only folded, one foot in front of the other, soles facing upward. Be sure the cushion is the right height, or it will be hard to keep the legs on the floor and the backbone straight.

TRADITIONAL POSTURE:

Also known as the Carmelite posture or the tailor's position. Place the knees on a blanket, the tips of the toes slightly covering each other, then sit in the hollow of the heels. The knees can be together or spread out. Many beginners use a cushion in this posture which they slip between the heels and the buttocks. This makes the position less painful. You can also use a small stool, or a wooden cube to sit on.

ON A CHAIR:

For those who find it hard to use one of the above postures, it is certainly possible to meditate on a chair. Do not lean back, but sit on the front edge, legs perpendicular to the floor, the feet parallel, so les firmly placed flat, or cross the ankles, with the knees always lower than the pelvis, otherwise the vital center is not freed up.

Every way of sitting requires a time of apprenticeship at the beginning. Our body, deformed by false attitudes which our sick spirit enforces upon it, will suffer in the first few months. A whole reconditioning must take place. The joints will hurt, but this suffering must not be useless. Accepted and felt from within, it will become the junction of the body and the soul and take its place on the Way to the unity we seek. Soon this effort to sit in meditation will become more agreeable, will easily last longer, and will be taken without effort.

It will have become second nature, or rather an opportunity for our true nature to express itself fully! As soon as we are seated, we will feel our whole being relax, and a sensation of well-being set in. To t he absolute immobility of the body will quickly correspond a surprising calm of the spirit and of the emotions. It becomes a true recollection in the deepest sense of the word. And eventually, this posture will reveal itself not only as that which is most restful, but as that which is most regenerative: open to t he mysterious forces of Being, we will leave our meditation with a new vitality.

THE HANDS

The way of holding one's hands is very important. They are in a way the prolongation of our consciousness. We can place them in different ways, of course, but you will notice, confirming thousands of years of experience, to what extent inner attention is increased when the fingers of the left hand rest on the fingers of the right hand, or vice versa if you are left handed. The thumbs, placed horizontally, lightly touch each other and form with the fingers a sphere, the symbol of the celestial world; the forearms rest on the top of the thighs, the sides of the hands in contact with the abdomen. It is most important that the shoulders fall normally in perfect

relaxation, the elbows supple. The whole creates a large cup, symbol of the inner cup, ready to receive that which must die and give birth to new forms of being. The magnetic field of this microcosm which is our body is thus closed by the hands and the feet: the energy can then circulate freely.

THE EYES

They are to remain, if possible, partly closed during meditation. This will seem difficult for those who are in the habit of closing them, but one can get use to this quickly. The masters say that there is practically no progress when we meditate with our eyes closed. Moreover, sleep can often take over, along with distractions of all kinds and daydreaming. Maintaining contact with the exterior world helps to stabilize the body. So, with your eyes half open, eyelids relaxed, a neutral look placed on a point approximately a yard ahead, we fix our gaze on nothing, letting our attention go inward.

THE BACKBONE

This is the most essential aspect of sitting in meditation. To sit up straight usually means for most of us sticking out the chest and holding in the stomach because we have lost our center of gravity and live on the surface of ourselves. This posture is taught in all the armies of the world and those other barracks we call schools. For violence is only possible (whether in scholastic competition or under gunfire) when we are expulsed from our Self toward the small and frightened self, where eliminating the other becomes the law of survival.

We must therefore rediscover the right posture with our center of gravity in the stomach. The simplest way, once seated, with our hands properly placed, is to lean forward, then reconstruct the vertical position from its base, beginning at the level of the coccyx, rising one vertebrae at a time. Coming to the head, we then pull the spinal column up and let it sit on itself, vertebrae on vertebrae, without sinking toward the bottom or becoming rigid at the top. The spinal cord is straight but supple.

THE NECK

The neck is a crucial area. If it leans forward or backward too much, it breaks the continuity of the vertical position and inhibits the descent into the self. In order to keep it in line with the spinal cord, you simply need to bring in the chin a little and not lose the contact between the top and back of the head and the ceiling or sky. Rooted in the sky, rooted in the earth, such is our constitution as human being.

THE LOWER STOMACH

It is this rooting in the earth which we must now work with. The vertical position rests on a foundation. As long as it is not solid, the rest is very fragile. Taking root in the earth depends entirely on a letting go at the top: we must first release and relax in depth in the neck and shoulders at the beginning of each expiration. This letting go of oneself is automatically followed by a great movement of confidence toward the lower: at the end of the expiration, we are literally sitting in our belly, which in its turn expands, relaxes, and roots itself deeper and deeper.

If the expiration is gently but firmly directed toward the lower parts, without any effort, the lower stomach will easily free itself. In prolonging the expiration at the end of its normal course, the abdominal inner wall is lightly tensed, which allows us to feel a force in the entire pelvic region. This stability of the whole is now unshakeable, in its center of gravity, and the whole person can now relax from top to bottom.

A LIVING SPACE

The proper vertical position is not rigid like a broom handle, but supple in a way which allows the spinal cord to gravitate around a fine point from which life arises. There is a simple way to find it which consists in moving back and forth several times with the whole of the spinal cord, in rhythm with our breathing. The movement diminishes progressively and stops of it s own in a space of several millimeters without ever losing either its vertical position nor the contact of the head with t he sky. In this little space, this mysterious point, we feel a true well-being, a life which invades the whole body from its center. If we are too far forward or backward, rigid at the top or slumped toward the bottom, everything is dead, as each person will quickly discover.

TRANSPARENT TO THE TRANSCENDENT

To believe that all this puts too much importance on the physical would be to hold to a deadly dualism of body and soul. It is true that centuries of spiritual ideologies and theological concepts have not helped us to live in the humility of our body! Yet it is through the body that I am: my body is myself, my way of being in the world. Even in the least gesture I can perceive something of my interiority, just as, inversely, any gesture, attitude or action has a profound influence on my inner universe and can become an occasion t o shape me on the Way.

The body therefore always expresses either a right way of being there, or a false way of being there. It is false when it inhibits, by all the tensions in the upper part of the body, the contact with Being and the possibility for Its manifestation; it is right when it allows a letting go of the dominating self and an openness to the fullness o f Being. If the exercise of the right attitude is properly followed, it leads to a "whole evolution of the person which signifies much more than a new way of holding oneself," writes Durckheim. "It is not a matter of a new physical attitude, but of a profound transformation of the person. Anchoring oneself little by little in a deeper foundation brings about a fundamental change. It expresses itself in a new way of seeing and accepting the world, in bearing suffering, in a new way of living...The Hara, the belly, opens an access to Being.

We are conformed to our essential being and fulfill it." This is an attitude of transparence before the transcendent, the awakening of a new consciousness which seeks to maintain this contact continually through the activities of daily life. We can take on the habit of living from this deeper center, whatever the circumstances, and it eventually becomes intolerable to give ourselves over again to the palpitations of the little surface self.

THE RIGHT TENSION

We only enter into the right attitude through the proper tension of the whole person through the body which we are. Right tension means a harmonious relationship between tension and relaxation. This is where we can best observe the difference between the body which we are and t he body which we have. There is a great gulf between saying "I have tension in my arm" and "I am tensed in my arm." In the first case, I relax the muscle and the feeling is solved by simple physical therapy; in the second case, I relax as a person and I then open within myself a new dimension which completely escapes the domination of the willful self. These are two different visions of what it means to be human and everything changes radically according to which one we are inspired by. Consider the enormous revisions in medicine and education under these new relationships!

THE TENSIONS OF THE BODY

A tension in one part of the body is always a blockage on the inner Way, for it reveals a personality distortion, a contraction of the self on acquired positions or a subconscious desire to affirm ourselves against our fears and insecurities. These kinds of tensions are innumerable, as varied as the circumstances of life and t he people we come upon. A trifle can throw some people into the most tenacious contractions: obsession, unappeased desire, resentment, irritation... Everyone takes their own particular poison. But whatever the tension, even the slightest one, it affects the entire person and inhibits transformation. "It matters little," says John of the Cross, "if it is a thread of silk or a heavy cord which holds the bird's leg, since it makes its flight impossible..."

Most of the time, it is an ensemble of tensions, more or less latent, sometimes very old, but constantly maintained, which forms the enclosure of a self forever preoccupied, centered in the top part of the body, far from any liberating confidence and begetting an utterly petrified existence. To relax a part of the body always means to let go of everything which is the expression of a person centered only on the egocentric self, and results in an increasing release from captivity as the contact with one's essential being is rediscovered. This contact is a slow but incessant maturation which is never fully completed. Inasmuch as I have learned to let go of all the tensions and fixations within, I witness the birth of a new form which must immediately be protected from the temptation of a new hardening through a letting go forever renewed.

That is how I enter into the wheel of metamorphosis where this maturation is characterized by a permanent transformation of forms which die and are reborn in the great movement of life, along the rhythm of the breath. If we live this process consciously, we are in this vivifying harmony of tension-relaxation which is the secret dynamism of all existence, carrying it to its ultimate realization through the manifestation of Being in all our attitudes.

Nothing will then stop us on the Way and each moment which presents itself is for us THE best occasion for progress. Life only takes on meaning in and through this continual maturing. Right attitude, proper tension and breathing form a whole, interpenetrating each other in a growing fusion which engages t he whole person on another level. Though they must be treated here separately, it must be understood that relaxation, as with these other actions, is not an exercise of the body which would do some good for the spirit but an entirely other requirement; only experience will confirm this.

THE EXERCISE OF RELAXATION

The techniques of relaxation are many. A fundamental element among all of them is FEELING. To receive a sensation in its pure state, without interpretation, creates an immediate disconnection in t he nerve centers, silencing the soul and the body. Psychosomatic research has obtained surprising results, healing neurosis of all kinds and even some paralysis. This is the scientific resurgence of the ancient but formidable intuitions of the Desert Fathers who came through the silence of body and soul to that "inviolable sovereign liberty" (John Cassian).

What does this mean for us? Once in sitting position, perfectly Still, become conscious of your breathing for a few moments. Breathe slowly and deeply. Then go through the whole body, from head to toe, by feeling from within one part then another and relax each place as you breathe out. This may seem difficult at first since the ability to feel in this way is completely atrophied in some people. But the capacity for interior perception refines itself very quickly and deepens at every session. Even if we feel nothing right away, the process of relaxation brings benefits from the very first attempt. This does not mean jumping quickly from one part of the body to another, but going to each part, from its surface to its depths, from exterior toward interior, and remaining there...feeling...and tasting the fullness of the sensation.

The result of this relaxation of the forehead, eyes and jaws is an almost invisible smile. It is a smile that we see on the face of saints and sages, and also on the face of the dead for they have finally completely let go. This interior smile must not leave during the whole meditation. Good relaxation of the tongue also affects the whole organism. Be sure that it is not tensed against the palate. Feel your tongue...Relax the throat, for it is often knotted up by anxiety or simply because we never cease speaking to ourselves. Let go!

Upon expiration, go to the back of the neck, that area so important for our interior development. It is there that the enormous tensions of our arrogant self go to crystallize, along with the tensions of the self which continually seeks to protect itself. You can feel this like a board between the shoulders or through a stiff neck as the Bible calls it. Let go of yourself from that false protection, open all that part of the top of the backbone right between the shoulders. Feel the relaxation... Then relax the shoulders by trying to feel them deeply from within, in all their length and breadth. This does not mean pushing them down mechanically, but simply letting go of yourself in the shoulder. Now feel the weight of the arms slide gently toward the elbows right into the forearms and the hands. Repeat the movement several times. Feel your arms getting heavier and heavier, warmer and warmer as they relax completely. Let go of yourself in the hands, inside the hands...

Afterwards, feel the two arms at the same time, from the neck to the hands like a big circle, always heavier and more relaxed with each expiration... Then, without ever sinking down, relax your back. On every expiration, feel the whole back dilate, relaxing on both sides of the spinal cord... Do the same in the chest. Feel it breathe...It is as if it opened in the center and everything expands and relaxes more and more. Feel it... Now feel the circumference of the belly area. Let it expand, becoming larger and larger, like the foundations of a pyramid. Let go of the lower stomach region...It is heavy, as though filled with lead, expanding... Feel the sitting position, the muscles of the buttocks...Then, as with the arms, feel the weight of the legs slide slowly toward the knees, through the calves, to the very ends of the feet...Feel your legs becoming heavier and heavier, warmer and warmer, relaxed... Repeat this movement several times, as needed. You can focus on each leg individually, as with each arm. This might be easier for beginners.

Some practitioners relax only the right arm and this relaxation, when it is well done and done completely, acts by osmosis on the rest of the body, revealing our interior unity. Once you have gone through your body, feel it all at once, from within. Relax completely as you breathe out, always in perfect immobility and with good posture. This exercise of relaxation can be done systematically at the beginning of each meditation. With the beginner, this will take perhaps fifteen or twenty minutes; but as you progress, it will only require a few moments. You need to begin with this effort, if you can, for our attention is in direct proportion to relaxation and it is this alone which allows the focus of our entire being. We now come to the doorway of meditation. The ways of approach are many. One must seek, experiment, and eventually everyone find his or her path, guided by their own inner force.

THE SENSATION OF THE DIVINE

Once we have attained a certain depth and well-being, t he exercise of relaxation can become meditation. It must not be reduced to a simple technique. As experience will show, it leads nowhere to consider the different parts of one's body from the exterior as objects and seek to relax them! We must develop the habit of entering into our body with all our consciousness, remain in the heaviness of our members a long time without resistance; there, we must taste the body that we are, perceive with all our being the profound change which slowly enters into our way of being present: the absence of boundaries, the exclusion of the dominating self, the unusual warmth of the body, the feeling of a mysterious Force which carries us and sustains us, the impression of total surrender. I no longer belong to myself and yet I am more myself than ever, intensely recollected in myself and yet connected to the whole universe...

This is an openness of our entire being to that which transcends it infinitely, as though we had responded to the secret but permanent invitation of the breath of the Spirit in the depths of our heart: "Ephatha, be opened" (Mark 7:34). Indeed, the depth of each sensation is a recreation of oneself, a veritable march toward liberty, that is, the awakening of the person beneath the ashes of the little self. Far from a simple muscular release, relaxation opens the doors of the inner mystery and offers the body as a place of covenant with God. "Behold, I stand at the door and knock; if any one hears my voice and opens the door, I will come in to him and eat with him, and he with me" (Rev 3:20)...."Offer your bodies to

God...The body is meant for the Lord...Do you not know that you are a temple of God?" (Rom 12:1; 1Cor 6:13).

But, if it is true that our body is the sanctuary of the divine Presence, we can say with saint Gregory Palamas that we are "flesh of His Flesh and bones of His bones..." God finally ceases to be "a ghost" for us, for we can now "touch him" (Luke 24:39)! We do not encounter him in abstractions or words: "Do not heap up empty phrases" says the Christ (Mtt 6:7), "Touch me!" (Luke 24:39). If he has in fact come out of the insurmountable Abyss which "no eye has seen, nor ear heard," it is precisely in order to become flesh and to assimilate himself to us so that we might "see His Majesty with our own eyes" (2Peter 1:16), "hear him with our own ears" (Mtt 13:9 and 16), "touch him with our hands" (1John 1:1), feel him with our whole being and let ourselves be seized by Him.

This meditation through feeling goes from the exterior toward the interior, from our surface toward our depths. The sensation is ephemeral: it appears and disappears, lasts only a fraction of a second, but like the wave is linked to the immense depths of the entire ocean. So too is the sensation linked to the infinite of our inner consciousness and, if we remain within it, leads us into the sensation of the Divine...the feeling of an ineffable Presence, a contact with Mystery which enters into the very least of our cells. As fire penetrates iron, the latter keeps its substance but becomes and realizes the fire which inhabits it and literally trans-figures it. This marvelous parable used for the first time by saint Macarius the Elder resonates through the Christian tradition, from East to West . Today as yesterday, Christ invites us to climb the holy Mountain and enter with him into the divine fire. Meditation concretely opens the path.

MEDITATION:

A PRIVILEGED PATH

It is in this context of life and death that we must trace a path. We are at the crossroads. And the decision for the journey can come only from persons or communities who have become aware o f the depths of their being and are present t o the adventure o f the twentieth century.

Both must be held together, for t his is not the time to run away in search of mystical comforts. The inner life is not a decadent complacency of the self or "bourgeois" luxury. We must look directly in the face of the realities of our time!

But how is this possible? Many believe that it is already too late to humanize the inhuman forces at work among us. In the light of historical facts as well as of our widespread neurosis, there is indeed no convincing reason to believe in the advent of a sudden mental mutation which would allow us to bring about an entirely different future. There are some who hope that biological progress will soon synthesize a hormone or an enzyme which will be able to heal our paranoid dispositions.

Will the salvation of humanity come out of laboratories? Will it appear on the shelves of pharmacies and be picked out by consumers? The day may not be far off when we will add the elixir of a mental stabilizer to drinking water so as to lower criminal behavior, to enhance the coordination of neurological circuits, to lessen conflict, and to normalize things.

But this would be criminal in itself, transmuting humans into passive robots. It would be naive to hope that drugs could regenerate the spirit, introducing something that was not already there. A revolution of an entirely different order is needed because humanity is of a different

order, and if we now face our greatest threat, we will be able to conquer it only by acts which are equally without precedence. Before such an extraordinarily new danger we need to find the source of the original and true creative power.

Today, we must rediscover ourselves in all our dimensions. Humanity's most heroic adventure is not the exploration of our external universe, however infinite it may be, but the journey toward our true nature. Infinity is found within us. Only from there will the world be re-created, for that is its origin: the inner force of humanity!

To survive, humanity needs a spiritual revolution. All the greats of our century converge around this point, believers and unbelievers alike. Nietzsche's Zarathustra was not the product. of a degenerate imagination but the first to observe that humanity must rise above itself. Einstein insisted on the transformation of human life in its totality, the necessity for conversion. Jaspers, another agnostic, went even further and did not hesitate to state that everything comes from the individual and depends on him. We have no other power than to draw from the liberty which rests in our depths. To dare to be an individual is to become transfigured in our relationship with our inner freedom, or, for believers, in our relationship with God. The emphasis here is not on the isolation of the self but on the intensity, the passionate interest of the self's relationship with God (or its being, its freedom), and through God, with others and the world.

This requires a permanent watchfulness. The place of this accomplishment is meditation, the kind which we will be describing here, exposing us to both the incessant movement of transformation within and genuine encounter with the outer world. This dialectic must be held together, otherwise we fall into a kind of suffocation of the self by the self or into a destructive rationalism. We might call it "active wisdom," liberating the extraordinary potential of our spiritual forces and finally letting surface all the happiness which inhabits us already.

This is what meditation aims at: creating a living person who sees God. The human being's masterwork is himself or herself. The word *meditation* does not mean here a reflection on a theme or on some rational thought process. Meditation is understood here as a *path of transformation*. It is a maturation of the entire person: in our relationship to ourselves; in our relationship to others and to the world; in our relationship to God; in the transfiguration within us of Absolute Being.

We therefore take the word meditation in its literal sense, *meditari* (*itari in medio*), which means being led toward the center. The center is not something toward which we concentrate, but something which concentrates us, uniting us from within, toward the interior. This center is essential Being, our transcendent kernel which is felt as a state in which the opposition of subject-object is dissolved. Such a state of relaxation is followed by the sensation of the birth of a new form. This is how essential Being itself makes its entry into our consciousness and is felt there as the vital center of a new awareness of the world. We feel as though we are newly born. Karlfried Durckheim. tells us that "this contact with Being begins with an almost unconscious yearning of the heart and must be followed ceaselessly, until we reach the fundamental experience of the explosion of self and t he realization of Being, which transforms everything."

MEDITATING IN THE BREATH OF GOD

We are born by receiving the first breath and die by giving up the last. Life is in the breath; it is the breath of life. Beneath our words is hidden the sin of division and the preeminence of the rational in our culture: soul, breath, wind, Spirit-so many different expressions, yet t hey are all contained in the Hebrew term *ruah*. The Bible has no complexes in speaking of breath, in opening at the same time the door to an abyss of mystery. And reciprocally, in speaking of Spirit, it does not fear expressing by that term the One who animates the very least breath in the nostrils of humanity!

We are far from these fundamental realities because we only see things in fragments, outside of their totality, reducing everything to a function. We have made of the most vital act, breathing, an institution by which we provide ourselves with air! While in fact it is the great movement of life which gives itself and recovers itself, a perpetual movement of transformation which, in one beat, gives birth to a new form of being and, in another, lets die the particular forms of our little conceited self.

It takes much practice to really understand that it is not we who breathe, but that Life breathes in us without our doing anything about it. When we feel this for the first time, it is one o f the most striking experiences of the great Force which inhabits us and maintains us in life without our intervention. We live only because the breath of God penetrates us constantly, as it penetrates all that exists; there is not a cell in our body which is not animated by this creative and vivifying Presence. Breathing can become a place of ineffable exchange, filled with Love. We must become conscious of this in meditation, not by fixing or analyzing, which would create a distance, but in joining with this movement of life, letting ourselves be seized by it, to be able to really hear in silence how each of our expirations, depending on how much we surrender ourselves in it, leads us to the hidden sources of our deeper being and there re-creates us in a new inspiration. This death-birth, this incessant movement, will progressively lead us into an indescribable fullness, and if we are faithful to it, essential being will invade us with its presence.

Correspondingly, inspiration is not a simple physical process, pumping in air, but a column of light, a kind of liberty in plenitude, which gives itself back as soon as it has reached its summit. Breathing goes from one pole to the other and encompasses the whole person.

We discover through t his experience a growing joy as we begin to feel our belonging to the Great Life which calls us into existence, maintains us in it, and can transform us com1pletely. In this potential is found our true freedom! Cut off from our roots, we live only from our artificial autonomy and no longer have this original confidence which gives Life. The self, always on the defensive, protects itself from all risks and tragedies: it surrounds itself with a thousand-and-one securities. So it is with our breathing. We seek to do it on our own instead of receiving it in a spontaneous and natural arising. We then appropriate it to ourselves, raise it toward the upper part of the body in the sphere of willfulness, and reduce it to being a little air pump.

The diaphragm, this great mediator of deep breathing, falls into immobility and atrophies. Our center is displaced toward the head and our breathing now comes only through the clavicle, the ribs, and the auxiliary muscles. This unconscious blockage of our breathing in the upper part of the body is of the same order as all the tensions and contractions which we have already mentioned: it is a distortion of the whole person, cut off from his or her depths. It is an obstacle on the inner Way, which only an always renewed letting go can overcome.

When we first observe our breathing, it is easy to see how difficult, if not impossible, it is at the beginning not to let our will, our self, interfere in an area which should not be under its dominion. The rhythm is soon broken, becomes irregular, often to t he point of suffocation! This is when we become conscious of the unnatural blockage of our breathing.

This is already a first step, even if it is humiliating. But it will be a long road to rebuild the bridges broken off from the deeper layers of our being, to rediscover the roots with this part of ourselves that is beyond the grasp of our will. The letting go must be such that all intervention of the willful self has to be eliminated, so that breathing can be done of its own, without resistance. In awaiting this event, which will be a giant step on the Way, we unconsciously continue to restrict our expiration, to stop it before it is completed, and to want to keep in a residue of air. This clearly reveals our fear of death, of expiring, and of sinking definitely into the anguish of annihilation. This fear of releasing the final breath inhibits us from waiting for a new inspiration to be given to us and receiving it with gratitude, freely, as a gift of love. We take it in lustfully, possessing it, "doing" it, instead of letting it be do ne. This is a manipulation of the movement of life and an obstacle to transformation. Simply consenting to expiration already represents a prodigious state of inner freedom; we give ourselves over, consciously and completely, to our death. The quality of each inspiration depends on the depths of our giving over of self, that is, on the capacity to become a new creature and to be utterly transformed. For most of us, only the final expiration will be perfect and will crown all the others, as the letting go and surrender of self will be complete. We then enter into the Life.

Our breathing is not an isolated function, but the expression of the whole person. A person's way of breathing expresses his or her general attitude toward life. This means that no breathing exercise will free us from inner blocks and be transforming if we do not radically change our attitude toward ourselves. I am my breathing. But to become conscious of it, other than from the exterior as an object, we cannot use our ordinary consciousness. Life is only discovered by living it from within. This means that the self must die and let go-and with it our habitual consciousness-in order to give birth, through meditation, to a new form of consciousness which, instead of observing and ascertaining, experiences life and breathing from within. We then know our breathing because we are literally born with it! We are our breathing in the true sense of the word, and to the extent that this inner perception becomes communion, it will profoundly transform us.

This birth opens us to our origin, there where we become ourselves and enter into genesis (John 3). Here we can receive and feel the power which comes from the depths of our being and understand to what extent we are strangers to ourselves. Opaqueness then gives way to transparence; the essential being awakens and becomes the true source of our blossoming. Our center is no longer in the head but in the depths. It is a consciousness-cup, intuitive, receiving, and perceiving everything with all the fibers of our being. Persons who live in this way find themselves on the Way, in a new vital impulse, a joy and freedom which lets them feel their belonging to transcendental reality. The sensation, then the experience, of Being are now possible, thanks to the death of the little dominating self.

We are there at the heart of all life: death-birth. This is the secret heartbeat inscribed in the essence of all creation and animating every living creature in a becoming which is always renewed. The different phases of this transformation are manifested in the rhythm of each breath.

When breathing is no longer deformed by all our tensions and can evolve naturally in a good relaxation of the body, its relationship is three-to-one. Expiration has three phases, the third one being situated between expiration and inspiration. Its profound significance is that which we have described and which must now be lived consciously during meditation:

(1) letting go - (2) giving oneself - (3) surrendering; then inspiration: (4) rebirth.

These are the four stages of the movement of metamorphosis, which are lived as a single impetus seizing our whole being, body-soul-spirit, to liberate it of all that inhibits its transparence and to allow the advent of the Wholly Other. With every turn of the wheel, each breath contains the whole density of the Way, which stretches across all of life and never ceases to deepen, to reveal its mystery, to allow new discoveries. In other words, the practice of meditation is a permanent exercise, a global attitude in daily life, where each occasion reveals itself as the best one to advance on the Way. Meditation is the only place where is fashioned the tool of continual vigilance, that which Durckheim called "the state of critical watchfulness." This is the "watch and pray" that Jesus spoke of. Indeed, we do not know "the day or t he hour" when Being will visit us, and we must watch continuously that nothing hinders its coming. This kind of "watchfulness" arouses in the experience of the present moment such a keenness, an acute sensitivity toward that which is false and blocks our advance on the Way, that it immediately provokes a letting go, through which all meditation begins.

(1) LETTING GO

After going through the body to relax it from head to foot, feel yourself for several moments throughout your body all at once. When the body is perfectly still, become conscious of how it breathes, the slow and deep movement of the diaphragm which comes and goes. Be a passive witness t o it. Seek to enter with your consciousness into the expiration, to unite with it in a way, consenting to it more and more, accepting it. The letting go takes place at the beginning of each expiration and occurs especially in the nape and the shoulders, the upper part of the body, during the whole length of the meditation. Let go in the shoulders. All our tensions are ultimately crystallized in this area where we are fixed and settled in our self. Let go. At the beginning of the expiration, you might say "let go" o r "I am letting myself go " as you feel it happen. We all know the exceptional power of a word repeated during relaxation. It increases that which we seek to obtain. But after several weeks or months of regular practice, a certain inner maturity will make us understand that we no longer need the expression.

We will prefer to live in silence, in a simple contemplation of our breathing. It is important to repeat that we must not let the shoulders fall, but let oneself go in the shoulders, let go of oneself as a person centered and contracted in this upper part of our body, letting go of all that blocks our inner evolution. This letting go is a true death to a particular I in order to live more fully. It is a burial, a journey through our inner desert, sometimes long and painful like all the Easters where we leave one way of life for another. But between the two we must undertake the journey, letting go until we are utterly stripped, until we have reached the realization of the beatitude of "the poor in spirit" (Matthew 5:3).

This is to become a poor person, whom Meister Eckhart described as "one who needs nothing, knows nothing, and has nothing." There is nothing to gain, nothing to lose. Nothing to give, nothing to take. Only to be here in all simplicity, yet wealthy with inexhaustible possibilities, being poor in the true sense of the word. All religious experience tells us this: to be absolutely nothing is to be everything. When we possess something, this something will keep all else from entering.

Meister Eckhart expressed this in a wonderful way:

"If a man is empty of all things, of all creatures, of himself, and of God, and if God could still find room in him to act, we would say: as long as this place exists, this man is not poor with the most intimate poverty. For God did not intend for this man to have in him a place reserved for [God's] action, since true poverty of spirit requires that man be empty of God and of all his creation so that, if God wants to act in the soul, it is the man himself who must be the place in which [God] acts. This is what God would like. For if God once found a person as poor as this, he would take responsibility for his own action, because God then acts in himself. It is here, in this poverty, that man recovers the eternal being which he once was, which he is and will be forever."

Is not Mary the prototype of such a person? She is full of grace because she has responded fully to the call which resonates throughout the Bible, from the days of Abraham-"Go , leave your country"(Genesis 12:1)-to the rich young man "If you would be perfect, go, sell what you possess" (Matthew 19:21). Only a complete letting go creates the unique condition for entering the kingdom, and no one can become a disciple of Christ without renouncing everything (Luke 14:33). For "it is easier for a camel to go through the eye of a needle than for a rich man to enter the kingdom of heaven" (Matthew 19:24).

With t his first st ep, we enter into this call in an intimate way. I must first feel in a very realistic way what is occurring in my body when I begin to let go of my security systems in which I have settled. This is what our father Abraham felt when he took his first step into the burning sands of the desert in order to leave everything behind.

(2) GIVING ONESELF

letting go of tensions within is automatically followed by a gift of self. Consciousness descends from its pedestal to enter further into the depths of being, accompanying expiration which ends in the lower stomach. The tensions and contractions in the body reveal a lack of confidence and fear in the face of life. They are the traces of innumerable repressions, sexual and otherwise, the sign of a closure to the cosmic and universal forces which inhabit and transcend us. From that perspective, is it an exaggeration to say that a contracted stomach is a major obstacle on the interior Path?

So you must let your lower stomach expand: it relaxes, takes root more and more in the earth with its weight, and allows the hara, the center of gravity, to take shape. As we have said, the abdominal wall can be slightly stretched and the expiration gently but firmly directed toward the lower parts without any effort. To do this, prolong the first two or three expirations. The sensation of being in our hara, of feeling this force, comes very quickly and progressively engenders a new attitude in us. But already, on the physical plane, the anchoring of the hara is a true liberation from the contractions of the body in all its parts, and there is a repercussion on our health on every level. Everything depends on the right attitude, the harmony of tension-relaxation, and breathing.

At the beginning of the experience, we cannot distinguish between letting go and giving of oneself. The relaxation in the upper part of the body is not necessarily followed by a relaxation in the lower part. They are two different stages. But with a little effort, and with the help of our nature which asks nothing better than to quickly return to that which it is, we will live these two stages in a single movement from the shoulders toward t he pelvic region. It is a movement of confidence which, because we are not grasping onto an artificial and exterior security, places us totally in the hands of that which we do not yet know. However, we do know through experience that this Life to which we give ourselves leads us into another dimension, beyond space and time, and that this new anchoring has nothing in common with our former absurd security measures! The basis of our confidence has been radically shifted; every day we discover other moorings to untie, and many who thought they were believers experience an authentic faith. "Whoever humbles himself will be exalted" (Matthew 23:12). It is this humbling, this descent into oneself, which must be done before the ascent toward God. "The more one wants to raise his house," said Saint Augustine, "the more he must dig his foundations. And he who digs his foundations is obligated to descend into the depths. Before rising upward, the house is plunged toward the lower" (Sermon 69).

(3) SELF-SURRENDER

This gift of self during expiration naturally culminates in surrender, the heights of relaxation between expiration and inspiration. It is an entry into the deep levels of being, there where our will no longer interferes and where all we can do is surrender. In the space of this short moment, seconds only, a dizzying mystery is opened to us. This is the moment of metamorphosis. We must now be present to this moment with our whole consciousness, feel the force in our belly as it descends toward the earth to take root, and again apply to this third stage the words "surrendering" or "I surrender myself."

If the willingness to breathe out becomes more complete and if relaxation keeps deepening through our letting go, the passage from expiration to inspiration will be imperceptible, to the point where the movement stops and we go out of time and space. All that occupies our usual consciousness has disappeared, and we are touched by our eternal dimension. Taste this moment, remain within it, even if it is still lived in darkness, for "the darkness is not dark to you, the night is bright as the day" (Psalm 139:12).

The less we let go above, on the existential surface, the more we are closed in our depths, the passageway is obstructed, and the life of Being is constantly repressed toward the subconscious. Cut off from the forces of Being, there is neither freedom nor truth for us. But in the measure in which the movement of letting go is amplified, an awakening to Being will occur, followed by its progressive entry into our consciousness, and finally the realization of a union with It which deepens the whole life through. All the hardenings of the existential self are dissolved and melted down, and a new self, a new creature (Galatians 6:15), can blossom from the contact with this source of life. The original unity of Being is realized, a creative unity, liberating, transforming, always in this triple Presence which we spoke of in preceding chapters:

•• an indescribable plenitude which renews the inner person,

•• a Light which gives meaning and form to everything,

•• an Energy which unifies beyond all solitude.

This is an astonishing experience, which can flood us suddenly in privileged moments of life or can penetrate us little by little during meditation. The mystery of this encounter of self and of God is absolutely unique in each person's consciousness.

(4) REBIRTH

Our return toward our Origin, the primordial silence from which life arises, will engender a new birth. It is a column of light, a freedom in fullness, liberated from our small self, its positions, masks, and insecurities. But we must know how to wait with patience. We need to remain in surrender until a new inspiration is given to us and comes of itself. I cannot want it, or take it, or provoke it without turning into an egotist again; for it comes from the One "in whom we live and move and have our being" (Acts 17:28). All that I can do is to open myself more and more to him, to dispose myself to receive him with gratitude!

The quality of inspiration, its life and luminosity, depends entirely on the death which has preceded it, just as the foliage of a tree depends on it s roots. Let the breath come naturally, without abandoning the roots. Feel the form which it gives you and give it back in a new letting go as soon as it has reached its summit. The risk of wanting to stay in the upper part and to settle in the acquired is always there. Here we must be very sensitive to the almost imperceptible passage from inspiration to expiration, an eternal moment filled with silence.

This stage of rebirth is the culmination of the three preceding stages, the verification of their authenticity, the criterion of all true meditation. Without the radical renewal of the whole person, continual and durable, we cannot speak of serious meditative experience.

The letting go of the self and the diving into the purifying fire of Being unify our forces around a new center . The heart of stone (Ezekiel 36:26) which hardens everything, fixes and objectifies, slowly becomes a heart of flesh who se essential characteristic is a growing capacity to love. "By this all will know that you are my disciples, if you have love for one another" (John 13:35). Rebirth in love is the sign t hat Another has touched us, filled us, and transformed us. It is a conversion which seizes us more and more as the experience progresses, the realization of *metanoia* (conversion) inscribed at the heart of the Gospel, the great turning of life without which there is no human or Christian maturity.

We now live in a way which escapes all calculations and provisions. To describe this state is impossible; it is as new as each breath which arises in inspiration. We can say, however, that to live from this inner center, and no longer from one's head, completely changes our relationships to ourselves, to the other, and to God. No true relationship is possible at the level of thought alone, where people are reduced to objects. The location of our deeper Self is a bottomless mystery and the one place where the only true revolution can happen, that of the self and consequently of the world! (See the Beatitudes and the writings of Francis of Assisi and Seraphim of Sarov.) "Being rooted and grounded in love ... you may have power to comprehend what is the breadth and length and height and depth ... that you may be filled with all the fullness of God" (Ephesians 3:17-19).

ON THE WAY

When you begin meditation, the temptation will be to create the rhythm yourself, to let go, to give yourself over, to surrender, to be reborn, imposing all this with your will or thinking it. But as relaxation deepens, the movement will evolve on its own. You become the movement and live it consciously.

This profound communion excludes little by little all duality: thoughts no longer trouble you, nor any other activity of the mind. In all centuries, spiritual persons have called this the silence of the spirit, and contemporary science names it alpha waves. Science is only confirming that which mystics always knew and for which contemplative meditation remains the best Path. If thoughts, images, distractions come to occupy our spirits, let them come, like the sounds which come to our ears or the light coming to our eyes, without resisting them, and especially without analyzing them. Simply return to the fundamental attitude: letting go--giving over-surrendering - rebirth. This will lead us into an extraordinary calm, and distractions, as the Orientals say, will pass by like clouds.

The exclusion of all mental activity, thought, or reflection is not the result of a voluntary effort. The intervention of will would be a tension which would falsify any meditative attitude. You must strictly not want anything. The more I want something, the less I will get it! It is the same thing with the good things that happen to us: don't stop at them, concentrate on them, or wish to hold them back, otherwise you will be deprived of them immediately. Don't grasp onto anything, either positive or negative. Don't seek to recover today the state in which you were yesterday; to want it is the best way not to get it. Simply sit down, relax, and take up the basics which have been formulated here. Always begin again. Let yourself be surprised.

It is perhaps useful to add, though it seems obvious, that at the beginning, the process of meditation does not realize itself with the intensity described here. Until everything is integrated and nature has retrieved its rights over our pathological deformities, we will have to go by stages. At one point, we will focus on letting go, which will take the whole time of meditation. At another time, we will focus on the descent into our center of gravity, or surrender, etc. Then we will progressively join one to the other until the movement is spontaneous. Some days, it will be difficult to get past the simple corporal level and the impression of going through something mechanically; on other days, we will enter into an inexpressible transparence. But every time, we will have truly meditated and progressed. Walking along a path in the woods, we may encounter stones, fallen branches, ambushes of all kinds. It is the same for the Path of meditation. Yet we advance nevertheless, and we never leave it without being different from the one who entered upon it.

Made in the USA
Lexington, KY
16 August 2010